A Matinée in Plato's Cave

A Matinée in Plato's Cave

Rob Griffith

Water Press and Media

A Matinée in Plato's Cave

Inquiries should be addressed to:
Water Press and Media
2004 Whitebridge Road
Argyle, Texas 76226

First Edition February 2008
Library of Congress Cataloging-in-Publication Data

Griffith, Robert, 1970 Jan 16.-
A Matinée in Plato's Cave: poems by / Rob Griffith.
p. cm.
ISBN-13: 978-0-9744524-6-3
ISBN-10: 0-9744524-6-7
LOC 2008921678

Covert Art by Hopper, Edward (1882-1967). *New York Movie*.
1939. Oil on canvas, 32 1/4 x 40 1/8". Given anonymously.
(396.1941) The Museum of Modern Art, New York, NY U.S.A.

Book and Cover Design by Water Press and Media
The text of this book is composed in Baskerville

Printed in the United States of America

Acknowledgments

Certain poems in *A Matinée in Plato's Cave* first appeared in the following publications to which grateful acknowledgment is made:

Another Chicago Magazine: "Still Life with Speculative Fruit"
Cottonwood: "Diptych"
The Dark Horse: "Summer Rain, Arkansas"
The Evansville Review: "It Takes so Little," "At the St. Louis Art Museum," "Gluggathykkn"
The Formalist: "A Fan's Proposal," "Alchemist," "Parallax," "Love Song in Grantham, England"
Kestrel: "The Baptist Croupier," "A Wedding Poem to Replace the One the Post Office Lost," "A Thursday Matinée in Plato's Cave"
Neovictorian/Cochlea: "Lincoln Cathedral"
New Millennium Writings: "So Here's the Poem I Promised," "All That is Green"
North American Review: "For My Cousin's Wedding st Theatre Memphis"
Oxford American: "Brucker Alone," "F-16 Crashes outside Strawberry Plains, Indiana"
Pavement Saw: "A Euclidean Heart"
Pivot: "Smiling at Flowerpots," "Two Hours before Holly Takes Him Back"
Poems & Plays: "Cashing It In," "Confessions"
Poet Lore: "The Myth of Infinite Possibility"
Poetry: "The Cartographer"
Prairie Schooner: "Wild Swan in Pool," "Broken," "Killing Delia"
Rhino: "The Synesthetic Food Critic"
River Styx Magazine: "Adam, after Eve," "Poisoning Caesar"
Talking River Review: "Death Comes to the Bookstore Café"
Twilight Ending: "Words like Water"

The poem "Still Life with Speculative Fruit" was the recipient of the *ACM* Literary Award for Poetry.

The poem "Kid Curry in Knoxville, 1902" appears in *Knoxville Bound*, an anthology of poetry about Tennessee (Metro Pulse Publishing, 2004).

The poem "Love Song in Grantham, England" appears in *Rhyming Poems: A Contemporary Anthology* (University of Evansville Press, 2007).

Some of these poems appeared in the chapbooks *Necessary Alchemy*, winner of the 1999 Tennessee Chapbook Competition (Poems & Plays, 1999), and *Poisoning Caesar* (Finishing Line Press, 2004).

For Tiffany

Table of Contents

A Gathering of Shades

Gardens and Firelight

One More Strange Island

A Gathering of Shades

Broken

Before September burned away and nights
Grew long and cool as tombstones, the pastor lit
The chapel's boiler, a gut of iron and fire
So choked with soot from harder years it coughed

Black smoke all through the church. The pastor, lost
Within this false night, staggered to open
High windows, let out the dark. He paid
To have the boiler fixed and cleaned, but soon

The rumor ran around the women's choir
That Pastor's check had bounced. Since June,
He'd played the church's cash on dogs and hit
Rock bottom. He hung himself in shade
Beside his house, the fields so full of light
He half-believed there was no such thing as sin.

Poisoning Caesar

By the time that spring had burst
and spent its green fury
on the jaundiced streets of Rome,
the deed was nearly done.

Every night, while Augustus slept
with slim-ankled courtesans
or boys bathed in jasmine,
wifely Livia slipped out, stole
across the courtyard, and climbed
into his fig tree's black arms.

By starlight, she lacquered every fig
with poison, singing softly and thinking
of all his quiet afternoons cradled
in the shade of trunk and fruit.

The figs he ate, she imagined
as fat, purple drops crashing
into his waterclock heart,
and she wondered every day
when the blood and nightshade
that swirled in his veins
would arouse an ecstasy
of trembling or heavy breath,
or, most desired, fill his lungs
with his body's own corruption.

Her own blood groaned
with secret venoms, she knew —
dusted on her roses, painted

on the lip of her favorite chalice,
or maybe traced into the contours
of rib, neck, or shoulder.
All she knew for truth
was that soon, one of them
would inherit the golden ruin
of love, this slow way of killing.

At the St. Louis Art Museum

— Mummy death mask, encaustic on wood, first century A.D.

Someone loved her once,
met her in deep, moonless gardens,
murmured into the plexus of neck
and shoulder words woven of breath
and a susurrus of reeds in wind.

When he calls, perfumed and oiled, so formal,
he knows the shape of her
beneath her simple cotton shift. She smiles,
the corners of her mouth winging up
like tiny sunbirds, like benedictions.

That smile is gone, and what's left is wood
and paint thickened with beeswax.
Nearly touching, we lean closer
to read the small print that explains
the chemistry of color — tinctures of green
malachite for eyes, umber creamed
with white lead for skin, and bone black
for hair — all spread carefully with brush
and blade. After two thousand years,
all that remains is that artful smile
and the faint smell of honey behind glass.

Already thinking of home, a light dinner,
and early bed, we step away and turn
toward the gift shop, our whispers echoing
like faint birdsong over broad waters.

For My Cousin's Wedding
at Theatre Memphis

— July 2, 2005

The curtain glides into the heavy dark
Above the stage, its black boards simply lit
By one pale spot. You enter, hit your marks,
And say your lines, those ones rehearsed just once

The night before despite the fact that this
Is it, the kind of play that takes your life
And sends it singing, staggering out to kiss
The future's hard, dark mouth. Behind the lights,

The audience holds its breath, imagines all
The bright, romantic backdrops you might fly down —
The patient, gothic stones of Heathcliff's hall;
Carrerra columns strong enough to hold

A trellis, plastic roses, and Juliet's
Bower; or Helena's glittering forest, a scrim
That cloaks the lovers, helps them to forget
The world that lies beyond the dreaming wood.

Still holding hands, you kiss and take your bows,
Then dash into the wings to pay the priest.
He trails behind, his surplice like the prow
Of some sun-bleached ship coming home at dusk,

Cutting through the gloom. Applause like rain
Tattoos the stage and dogs you as you run
The gauntlet to your car. You clutch your train

And slam the door, the silence like a bell jar.

But while you've left your audience behind
To drink too much, eat canapés, and dance
Beneath the chandeliers until we're blind
With light and wine, remember that we're here,

We're always here — a pack of gray faces
That trembles just beyond the edge of sight,
A silent chorus watching from those places
Untouched by sun. And when you're on the lake,

Cloaked in blue air and squabbling over sunblock;
Or when you're in your kitchen, washing cups
And talking in the still beneath the clock;
Or when, both dressed in Sunday best, you go

To wedding, wake, or shower, we're there
To help you strike the set and sweep it down
To bone. And in the house lights' dark glare,
You'll kiss again, and know you're not alone.

F-16 Crashes outside Strawberry Plains, Indiana

— May 17, 2004

His chute still furled but trailing as he drops,
He is an exclamation point plunging
Down the sky's blue page, his smoke-wreathed jet
A pencil smudge arcing off the margin
To crash across the Wabash. Letters unsent,
A woman leans against her mailbox, numb
With fear, and watches as his silhouette
Is swallowed up by fields of early corn.

And even though he falls no further off
Than fifty yards or so, she hears no sounds
Except her own hot pulse within her ears
And the ceaseless wash of summer breeze —
That machinery of May that breathes and hums
As if to say that nothing new could happen.

Death Comes to the Bookstore Café

He ducked between Religion and Self-Help,
vulture-hunched over a copy of *I'm OK – You're OK*.
I might not have even recognized him —
no black cape or scythe; no pale bones shimmering
beneath the cowl like moths in moonlight;
just another doughy teenager sausaged
into black slacks and a cheap white shirt,
the ubiquitous uniform of waiter, clerk, or busboy —
but when he dipped the book's wings
to glance around the store, I glimpsed the Omega,
the Greek letter embroidered across his apron
like an upside-down urn or a golden bridge
so ridiculously arched that no one could cross.
Or maybe it was simply his nametag, DEATH,
that tipped me off, spelling out in block letters
mysteries I thought folded in the wings of dark angels.

He prowled the edge of the bookstore's café
(a temple of chrome, sea-green glass,
and hardwood floors the color of buttered toast)
where a poet with crow-dark eyes
leaned across the lectern and into the sparse crowd
and strained to be heard over the chuffing espresso machine.
She launched epiphany after epiphany into the air:
love is sweet; mortality defines us; death is democratic;
and I could imagine the ideas as golden birds
that leaped, fluttered once or twice, then dropped,
beak-first, into coffee cups, pieces of cheesecake,
and the laps of bored customers.

As she read, she stared at this prosaic Death
and followed him with wild, moonish eyes

as he shambled into the café and ordered a Diet Coke.
But her affection went unnoticed
as he sucked his ice and sized up the waitress,
whether for the grave or something more salacious
I couldn't say. But when he rose to leave, he paused,
still bent over the table like a question mark,
and scribbled a note or maybe his phone number
on the bill. He scurried outside, lurked,
and struggled to peer back through the plate glass,
his breath curling away in gray feathers.

When the waitress cleared the table,
pocketing the bill without a second glance,
he turned away and plodded after the dim shapes
of departing customers. The poet was saying something
about the depredations of love
and the promise of loss in everything.

Killing Delia

Humped beneath the comforter, she snores
enough to crack the house. In the dining room, the plates
shake in the cupboard, the fragile glass
and china shiver with each breath, and he thinks again,
"I can't get this diesel off my hands."
He drifts to sleep, the sound rubbing his bones like a cat.

He dreams of slim women and cool skin
then wakes and slogs into the kitchen, his glance sliding
off his wife's bulk. Wrapped in terry cloth
the blue of glaciers, she smiles into her shoulder, turns
the bacon with an upside down fork.
Rat poison? Sleeping pills like babies' teeth in her grits?

The seeds of apples hide cyanide.
How many would he need to crush with mortar, pestle?
"Would you stay and hold me for a bit?"
she asks and puts his plate before him. He nods and dreams —
a thousand red and perfect hearts, cored
beside the back porch, rotting in shade and a blank sun.

The Baptist Croupier

Brucker dreams of bones.
Teeth like wobbly dice,
pale coins of knuckle,
and thorns of shattered wrists.
Each piece dredged from the lake
and pressed into his palm
by his drowned brother's hands.

Tonight, stars stagger up the sky
while casino neon and dusk's coal fire
burn over the treeline.
His brother's shade shambles
out of the oxbow's black water,
a dank sack of rags and flesh
who counts out twelve full moons
with fingers dark as cypress.

Brucker leans into the smell of silt,
strains to hear him speak or breathe,
as lake water drips into silence.
He wonders how long,
how long before the dead sleep.

Waking in cool bed sheets,
Brucker sloughs off dreams
with a shave and hot shower.
He surrenders to the day
and heaves himself into slacks,
a starched shirt, and a silk vest
the color of spring clover.
He adjusts his lapel pin,

a silver shamrock,
and hopes its glint blinds God.

At church, he sits in a dream of light.
Stained glass drenches him rose and blue
while the preacher's words roll
like a rumor of thunder over open fields.
His mind closes to the sound
like a violet to rain.
As the collection plate passes,
he steals two quarters,
turns them over and over in his palm.

Before work, he flips the coins into the lake,
watches them arc over the water,
and sees each one frozen, briefly,
against a bright bath of light and grief.

Kid Curry in Knoxville, 1902

His saddlebag, fat with stolen rings and pocket watches,
clanks against his back as he lopes across the freightyard,
its rails and gravel shrouded in ankle-deep, October snow.
This is two years before he'd kill a cop on Market Square,
two years before they'd hunt him down,
crack his jaw and ribs with bullets, and leave him
beneath a naked dogwood listening to the voluptuous clock
of his own unwinding pulse. This time, he gets away.
The jeweler he pistol-whipped and robbed,
a wattled German who had tried and failed
to fix his father's watch, still lay behind his smashed-in cases,
the shards like bits of ice across his beard and chest.
Curry hopes they won't find the shallow-breathing body
until he's hopped a train to Asheville or Charlotte.
Between the freightyard and the river,
he hides beneath a magnolia and listens as the snowflakes
tick against the leaves and kiss the water, relentless and faint
as the hiss of a thousand second hands.

Cashing It In

People are cashing it in
all over — the man
who tailors his final suit
from salmon skins, then swims
a cold, Pacific stream,
his shoulders a scaly glint
as he goes singing
to call the bears downstream;

the third-shift worker
who locks himself
in a beef freezer in Texas
on a holiday weekend
and uses this end of time
to chalk himself,
to show his own rib eye,
roast, and tenderloin;

or the woman who rolls
herself in her Persian rug
that smells of dog and popcorn
then wonders how to lift
herself over the guardrail
and into the lake
without coming undone.

Grief comes flowering,
the tailor's wife would say
to no one in particular,
like azalea and foxglove
against a snowbank,

orange and lemon reflected
in the dark mirror of a river
clogged with rafts of ice.

Even in this cold,
we are fools
to wear our loneliness,
to watch this woman
fill her pockets with stones
and wade into the flood
like an actress striding offstage.
Chin high, shoulders draped
in silk and light, her arms filled
with paper roses,
she carries only props
into the dark wings.

Two Hours before Holly Takes Him Back

He leaned his guilt into the sunflower
Glow of the early morning Waffle House
And thought again of touching her thin blouse,
Its cotton twined and roped with a shower
Of printed thistles. Bruises in the bower
Of neck and mouth had blackened her hothouse
Smile, marred her fragile face. He ate, then drowsed
And dreamed of granite hands, their hard power
Caressing pale skin, crushing the flutter
Of pulse that flailed wildly beneath the press
Of stone. Her battered flesh unfurled, and vines
Like claws embraced his hands and face, stuttered
About his throat and died. He woke depressed
And hungry, vowed to say he'd change, given time.

Adam, after Eve

After grief, alone again with the world,
he finds those little pleasures, so long misplaced,
turning up like unlooked-for coins
in pockets or the bottoms of drawers.
Shuffling in the morning kitchen,
piles of fig leaves on the bedroom floor
and stacks of dirty plates and cups rising
from the sink like a miniature Babel,
he picks up a dish brush dripping with soapy water
and stares at the bristles. The only words
that come are "hairy teeth," and he turns
to ask Eve for the word he's lost.
But all that is left of her is emptiness,
a dull ache in his side on rainy days.

He knows that other words are escaping too,
flying south like the blackbirds
stitched across his autumn sky,
and he knows that soon he will forget
the names he shaped, like urns, to hold his fears.
And when their clay cracks and crumbles,
he knows that *wolf* will become *hunger*,
water will become *cold beast*,
and the clematis outside his kitchen window
will become *slow destroyer* —
word by word, the world uncreated.

But this too, he thinks, is wrong,
for he suspects that, nameless or not,
the waxwings will still settle
in the tall grass, the dogwood

will catch fire every spring,
and the wren outside his window
will sing as always.

Gardens and Firelight

Still Life with Speculative Fruit

*— For Robert Frost, Billy Collins, and all those
other poets who own nice things to meditate upon*

I don't have a pear orchard
bordered by low, fieldstone walls
to contemplate in moonlight,
so I can't walk onto my back porch,
its tightly tucked bricks sweating
through an August night,
to see how each pear seems poised
at the end of a slightly bent branch.

And I can't slip back inside the house,
sit at the kitchen table, and measure
the meaning of a perfect bowl of oranges,
yesterday's folded paper,
or the glazed blue clay of the salt shaker —
each object anchored to the tiled counter
as if it were the only still point
in a universe of change.

I can't even retreat to my study,
slippered feet sliding
on the polished parquet floor,
to collapse in a teak and leather armchair
and read Ovid or St. Augustine
while my fingers dangle over a bowl of walnuts
placed within convenient reach
on a mahogany end table.

No, at four in the morning, I sit
beneath a bloodless fluorescent,

stare at a cracked desert of harvest gold Formica,
and listen to the whine of the refrigerator.
All I have is a blank notebook,
a thin stub of pencil, and an empty soda cup,
its wax scored with nail marks —
but no coffee, no bottle of cheap bourbon,
not even a cigarette or jigger of gin
to romanticize the scene.

And when I finish and go to bed,
I won't climb any stairs to a beautiful woman,
won't burrow under a down comforter
and kiss her neck, and we won't watch
as snow outside the window dismantles the world.

Alchemist

Those unguents, jells, and sprays; those powders, creams,
And dusts — I know so little how she makes
Herself become herself each morning. Paints
Applied to lashes and lids eclipse the moon
Of flesh beneath each eye, and she forsakes
The art of nature for a bag of tricks.
The dog, awake and patient, follows her
From room to room and watches as she works
To make her transformations. Bored, he leans
Against her thigh, his ears twitching with each click
From bottle, jar, or tube. There's no complaint
From him or me as she turns her back and swirls
The blush against her cheek. Like spellbound goons,
We love the mystery of her every quirk.

So Here's the Poem I Promised

to your neck and to that tufted mole behind your left ear
as we danced at the high school reunion,
where I learned that a dream deferred
sometimes wears too much makeup
and drives a purple El Camino.

We stole some plastic cups and a pint of gin
from the cash bar, banged through the emergency exit,
and drove my rusting Monte Carlo away
from Woodland Hills' manicured greens
into fallow fields of sedge and cotton.
I edged the car through a sigh of chest-high weeds
and stopped beneath an oak's skeleton.
But you know all of this — you were there,
chattering about romance and missed opportunities
while you hiked your skirt and spritzed your thighs
with a breath of *Tabu*.

Before the tick of the cooling engine counted ten,
we tumbled into the back seat like lemmings,
the compulsions of tongue and touch swelling
to fill the car, obliterate fields of night and time.
I think I told you something about your eyes,
how they held summer storm clouds
and flecks like flights of rust-colored thrushes
flushed from hiding by first lightning.

But what I really thought
was that they looked like mismatched marbles,
and I waited to hear their glassy click
when they rolled back in your head.

I wondered when my shocks would blow
as the car bucked, tires gripped by stems and briars
that raked their sides like lover's nails.
Near the end, you twitched,
and kicked off the window handle
as the car groaned one last time
like a ship breaking up on a reef.

We lay tangled in apricot taffeta
and gulped cold gin from the bottle
while the moon rolled past the back window.

Sometimes, words are too much
and crack the fragile skin of love's illusion.
You asked, *What are you thinking?*
and I was fool enough to tell you
about the marbles and the shocks,
knowing all along
I should talk about the moon.

Love Song in Grantham, England

"Words are signs of natural facts."
— *Ralph Waldo Emerson,* Nature

Without the names of the flowers, trees, or birds
That populate this tranquil, foreign place,
He walks the autumn fields, devoid of words

To tell her how he feels. It would be absurd,
He thinks, to try describing her lovely face
Without the names of flowers, trees, or birds

For apt comparison. Her lashes, blurred
By wind to grasslands gold and brown, grace
Their walks in autumn fields. Devoid of words,

He smiles and talks of nothing, hopes she's heard
What's not been said. There will be no embrace
Without the names of flowers, trees, and birds

To make his poetry. Love-struck, deterred
By nature's blank stare, he knows the waste
Of walks in autumn fields, devoid of words

To touch her heart. His love song goes unheard,
He talks in circles in his futile chase.
Without the names of flowers, trees, or birds,
He walks the autumn fields, devoid of words.

Parallax

The English dawn trembles behind the poplars
And drowns the stars, one by one, in milklight
As I walk out across the heath, scattering
Rabbits and one startled lapwing, which dopplers

From left to right and back again in fear.
The pond beside the house is still, reflects
A sky as grey and soft as wool, and only
Venus — that bright, cold chip of ice — appears

Upon the surface. Four thousand miles away,
You sleep, and when you wake in that silk night
Of Midwest heat and see a smattering
Of stars, they'll look the same, but in array
They're slightly changed. You too — your eyes, your neck,
More lovely with distance and lonely skies.

A Euclidean Heart

Bars of light slip between the blinds
and curve into the dimpled rises and clefts
of sheets, painting a woman's bare legs
the color of chalk. As she breathes,
he watches the subtle attack and retreat
of shadows across her back
and knows that she is still awake by the tight lines
of muscle in her neck. Dimly seen,
the phosphor hands of the nightstand clock fall
away from the moment of the argument
and drag the night forward in silent geometry.

Lying in a shroud of half-light,
he thinks of someone else, wants to reconstruct her
smile on a canvas stretched and primed,
ready to take the caress of horsehair and oil paint.
With dabs of oystershell blue for eyes
and long strokes of flax for her hair,
she'll stand against a scrim of thunderheads
in a sundress stitched with columbine,
her feet obscured in tufts of sawgrass.
He wants the world to be simple —
a collection of shapes and patterns
that intersect in predictable ways
and unveil the heart's contradictions.

Beside him, the woman wedged between light
and shadow pulls the sheet over her legs.
He wants nothing more than to break
through the frail canvas of each wall,
to touch the other's wrist
and feel the slow music of her pulse.

It Takes So Little

A girl across the street applies eye shadow
in strokes green and slow as tide,
and something gives way in my chest
like a plot of soft earth collapsing
beneath the foundation of a house.

Another slides my change across the counter
with slender fingers, pale as sycamore,
and I begin to think desire
is everything I'll ever own.

It takes so little — a word breathed
more than said, the graceful arc
of eyebrow or ear, a knifeblade
of perfume — every gesture perfect,
equal measures loneliness and hope.

This cold April, I walk in the park
and see bumblebees sheathed in ice,
frozen to drooping cherry blossoms.
Sun glinting off their icy caskets,
they cling to what they love so desperately.

The Myth of Infinite Possibility

From the rusted casket of his Chevy Nova,
the man with heavy shoulders waits for his wife
and watches women leave the grocery store
with paper bags and plastic sacks
filled with things for lovers or quiet meals alone.
His heater huffs dry air over his hands,
paints sunsets across cheeks and nose,
and clears a patch of frost from each side window.

A dark-haired girl with moonlight skin walks by,
wearing a sweater the color of thick cream.
Her long, red nails flash like tracers
in the clear, autumn air,
and she seems as remote and sharply etched
as distant mountains on a cold day.

As she passes, he smoothes back his thinning hair
and changes the radio station from NPR to rock 'n roll,
just in case she looks, just in case she hears.

He watches her reflection
in the black curve of a Coke machine
and notices how the plastic warps her image.
He thinks how time and light
make jokes of us all.

He presses a button on his aging radio
and feels the tuner slide back to its accustomed groove.
A steady patter of quiet talk dribbles
from the speakers, and he wonders
what would happen if he just drove off,

if he just kept going.
Would anything be different?

He thinks it wouldn't.
He'd simply find himself somewhere else,
in front of some other grocery, waiting for a different wife
who still shops for the same paper towels,
small jars of minced garlic, and steaks
with just the right amount of marbling.
And he'd be watching some other dark-haired girl
emerge from the bright lights of the store,
wondering if all escapes are accounted for.

Wild Swan in Pool

From our kitchen window, I can see the pond
Just down the street, a shallow saucer filled
With algae, ducks, and one lone swan
Who paddles circles all day long, pausing

Only to dip for fish and shake a spill
Of droplets off. His mate left him years ago
After some local dog ripped away his wing,
And now he sweeps across the pond unpaired,

Alone. I say, "They mate for life, I know,
So why'd she leave him there, and where's she gone?"
And while I talk, I rub my wedding ring
And watch my wife tuck a strand of blonde
Behind her ear. She smiles and says, "Because —
The world is hard. Just be careful on the stairs."

All That Is Green

This halogen morning, we'll take you
to a clinic where no one leaves whole,
where your mother will fill out papers
that detail her sexual history,
her current address, and whom to contact
in case of an emergency.
Her life's minutiae reduced to blue ink
on a photocopied page,
she'll avoid the nurse's eyes and pay cash.

In another room, she'll put on a paper gown
and place her feet in stirrups
while nurses ask about allergies.
I'll sit in the waiting room and twist
bits of paper, rub my hands across my jeans,
and glance at the second hand
of the moon-faced clock. Your heartbeat,
like the tick of a pebble in a cold creek bed,
will slow and come to rest.

Outside, dogwoods bloom white
as bridal lace, petals arcing
backward into their own desiccation,
and irises purple as bruises
stoop under the weight of morning sun.

Right now, I sit at the kitchen table,
concealed in the commonplace of a newspaper,
and try to hold myself as still as possible.
The slightest move and this moment,
like a fragile vase, might tip

and shatter across our floor.
My skin as white as bone,
I wonder at our calm.

You will know only the dark warmth of your mother
and the pain of separation by surgical steel.
She drags a smile across her lips and whispers,
"Relax. It's just like pulling a tooth."
But for me, time has folded
like the sun-battered petals of the iris,
and I can see our trip home through all that green,
all that returns from memory
in the wreckage of every spring.

Leaving by Train

The platform, long and black against the green
Surrounding hills, shines with pools of rain
That cast back the clearing sky in cold,
Uncertain blues. Alone, he stands and waits,

The quiet morning gone, the 10:15
A dream of steel and light not yet arrived.
Though barely spring, delphinium and rue
Burst along the verge, their crowbar roots

Crowding every fissure, every crease and fold.
He wonders why his heart, a paper hive
Long empty, remains immune to change
While the whole prismatic world dissolves. The shoots
Of tulips tremble in the breeze, still freighted
With rain. He shuts his eyes against the view.

A Cantabile of Regret

There's nothing harder than the letting go
Of love you left for fear. The bright tableaux
Of days and nights together break upon
Those quiet breakfasts under drapes of sun
And drown the heaving heart in undertow

Too cold to bear. There will be nights, I know,
When all my dreams will be of hard rowing
Through the shattered music of seas undone —
There's nothing harder —

And I will breast the tide and icy floe
To kiss your neck, a slow adagio
Of pulse singing along your veins. I'll shun
Those other lovers, bend my thoughts to none
But you, and drink your flesh like melting snow.
There's nothing harder.

Necessary Alchemy

Start with an observation:
Trout curve like ceramic ribbons
under glass, pure
mechanicals in cold water.
Her hair is coiled copper
behind silver pins. Potential
balked by gaps
too wide to jump.

Love adheres to the laws
of thermodynamics, motion:
an object at rest tends to remain
listless, lonely until acted upon.

We need an alchemy
to transform the self,
grow tongues in midnight gardens,
sluice the body down to bone.

Summer Rain, Arkansas

We fished until the light was swallowed up
In cattails, until our cobweb lines had dimmed
Against the sloe-black pond, and then, fed up
With empty hooks, we headed home. Loose-limbed

And tired, I climbed into the car while Dad
Broke down our rods and packed away our gear.
Our headlights piled the dark against the sad,
Cruel edge of Highway 64 and seared

The center lane with white. I slept, then woke
To find a rain-slick road, now cooled and steaming.
And soon the frogs came out, like some baroque
Parade. The shocks fluttered with each bump, streaming

Skin and blood against the car. The night
Spun on. I stared ahead and held on tight.

A Thursday Matinée in Plato's Cave

Perhaps a re-release of *Casablanca* would seduce us
off our mountainside, give us reason
to duck out of a brutal June afternoon
and take refuge beneath cool shoulders of stone.
And after the world had shrunk enough
to thread its way through our sun-strangled irises,
we'd find our seats, kick the shackles and coils of chain
to the sticky floor, and slip our smuggled champagne
into the drink holder between our seats,
the bottle's neck made green and limpid
by the light of coming attractions.

After the trailers stagger off the screen,
the cave's ancient speakers pop and hiss,
a burr of wasp wings behind each upholstered grill
(*insectum ex machina*).
You cross your ankles on the seat in front of us,
and your skirt slides back to mid-thigh
to reveal the glass stem of each leg.
You dip into your purse, pull out popcorn
bootleg as moonshine, each handful of kernels
a cluster of marigolds rising to your mouth.

You watch the movie, and I watch the light
graze your arms, your legs, your neck,
as the reel spins itself down to nothing,
loosing phantoms to flit across the screen.
The film ticks the world forward,
and bubbles and bits of fiber scuttle across each frame —
imperfections smoothed by the illusion of motion,
the persistence of vision — the way a bit of blue phlox,

stolen from the hillside, surrenders its incandescence
to your smile. But this, of course, is the problem:
the basic inability of parables or poems to reveal our full flesh,
to show anything more than cerements of light.

One More Strange Island

Solipsism

On these limpid winter mornings,
the sun is a greasy, golden smear
against my bedroom window,

and the gentle roll of old glass
casts puddles of straw-colored light
across the floor. It's easy to lie here

beneath a trellis of cold air and light
and to think the world ends at wall or sill.
Even the birch outside the window,

its bark shagged in bands of black
and silver, seems only a pantomime,
a mummer who taps the roof

while his chorus, a stand of sapling ash,
sways and moans behind him
in dramas of simple shadow.

And meanwhile, somewhere on the Atlantic,
there's a storm that cracks the sea
and rocks a boat of fishermen.

Below deck and wrapped in pea coats,
they huddle under a bare lightbulb
and listen to a woman sing on the radio.

From the weave of static, her voice peeks out
like moonlight from behind a stack of clouds,
and for a moment, the drum of waves

and the heavy smell of perch fade,
and those men become nothing but song,
silver threads that slip between the planks

and dash over piles of broken ocean,
tracing their way to the realities of home:
a blue teakettle, a woman in a bathrobe,

or maybe the bare limbs of winter trees
that catch and cast the sun in lightning jags.
Like those men, I'll have to leave my dreaming

and face the world. Climbing out of bed,
I'll wince against the cold of hardwood floors
and dress quickly in the morning's quiet,

leaving behind only your breathing,
the soft sound starting and pausing
like surf consuming the shore.

Smiling at Flowerpots

Lined with birches, the road was slashed by virgules
Of shadow, and sitting on my porch steps,
I waited for the autumn air to clear,
To sharpen every nib of grass, and limn

Each leaf with light. Staring across the street,
I thought I saw an Irish Setter sleeping
Beneath the neighbor's porch, and if I thought
I saw each copper hair, each inky whisker,

Or every heavy, dreaming breath he took,
I think I can be excused for smiling,
For letting my imagination form
A dog from the fact of brick-red clay.

Like tildes on an empty page, blackbirds
Are sliding south across the sky. The heart
Attempts to cleave the world to mind, this lens
Of air and light that lies behind the eyes.

Lincoln Cathedral

Pinning the sky against the dome of heaven,
It rises above the town, its yellow stone
Drabbed by centuries of soot and made
More plain with corbels, piers, and arches
Composed of local Ancaster grey. Its vaults,
Inside, contain what seems the whole of space,

A series of echoing chambers spaced
Along the nave — the nautilused mind of heaven
Singing for and to itself beneath a vault
Of empty, blue September sky. The stone
Gargoyles that line arcades along the arches;
The demons, saints, and friezes which were made

To frighten and to edify — all were made
By master craftsmen's hands. There's even space
Behind the fleshy curves and tiny arches
Of every carved eyebrow and lip — a heaven
Of angels' faces and forms all turned to stone
Above the choir, though each seems ready to vault

Away from earth and toward those perfect vaults
That lie beyond our sight. Yet what was made
To mirror God's perfection in light and stone;
What was made to bridge the awful space
Between God and man, earth and heaven,
Is flawed, imperfect. Those who stretch and arch

Their necks can see loose keystones, arches
Just left or right of plumb; and those high vaults
Which frame the lancet windows' scenes of heaven

Are not always quite aligned or true. Made
By fathers, sons, and grandsons, the spaces
They created from faith and local stone

Are imprecise. Apprentice carvers, stone
In minds and hands, stood beneath the arches
And worked on practice quatrefoils, the space
They left between leaf and bloom — like tiny vaults
Themselves — their proof of mastery of made
Things and readiness to rise to the heavens

Of clerestory and light-bathed vaults.
These stones and empty spaces, arches made
Of imperfect prayer, fall too short of heaven.

The Synesthetic Food Critic

"Their roasted duck, basted with butter, cloves,
And garlic, tastes as light and sweet as wine
Uncorked from ancient cellars," I write, although
Of course, I haven't any clear idea

Of how the fragrant meal would taste to those
Whose tongues and brains are wired in better ways.
To me, the cooling duck and spinach salad
Are trapezoids and purple thorns that prick

The flesh behind my ears like the tines
Of cocktail forks. How can I write that, or say
To women, "My God, your perfumed neck flows
Like Brahms across my tongue?" They're always quick
To raise the lights, recall a place to be.
I'm cursed by lying words, a clumsy palate.

A Wedding Poem to Replace the One the Post Office Lost

In a field softened and combed by winter floods,
Feathers of snow are falling, shrouding ground
And sheathing limber pines with frost, while huddled
Postmen drink rye from paper cups around
A reeling fire. Hands gloved in wool, they feed
The flames with sacks of letters, Christmas cards,
Some glossy junk mail, and postcards that plead
For reconciliation. All are charred,
And flakes of incandescent paper rise,
Go nova in a brittle breeze, then cool
And fall to pepper fragile sheets of ice
Already daubed with bottle caps and fruit
From pillaged baskets. For you, I wish for fire
To bridge the void, lift love above the embers.

Brucker Alone

Crossing the Hernando Desoto bridge
at night, the Mississippi a slow ache
beneath the trestles, she left quietly
for Little Rock. Quietly, too,
our love left a while back, unnoticed
as the friend at a crowed party
who takes a long last draw of cold beer
then steps into the dark without goodbyes.

At sunset, the river is a mask of light,
gold and red, but it's nothing
to me now — just a brown dog leg
that humps the Memphis skyline.
On this side, there's nothing
but empty voices, the clatter of glass
and silverware from the doors
of open kitchens, and hollow blues
ghosting down alley after alley.

On the other side, there are fields of rice,
oxbows filled with catfish, and a sky
sewn carefully to the flat horizon.
In spring, the earth rushes to fulfill
its own promise in brown and green,
the promise of nothing more
or less than simply going on.
It's enough. Mostly, it's enough.
But I'll be goddamned
if I'm not dreaming of Arkansas.

A Fan's Proposal

During the seventh inning stretch, he knelt
On the dugout and proposed while people drank
Their beers and grazed on popcorn, hotdogs, chips,
And ice cream. Amplified, his voice unwound

From every speaker, distance shearing words
From lips, while showers of pointillist hearts
Cascaded across the scoreboard, hounded
By neon cupids. Later, over glasses

Of beer at the Gerst House, he grinned and held
Her hand while toasts were made and friends played darts
Or pool. He talked about their plans, the sounds
Absorbed in barroom smoke and pints of Bass.
A wedding like a carnival. Her blank
Expression too elusive to be bound.

Isabel Returns to Selmer, Tennessee

They stalked her with their eyes,
those sad-eyed guys with comb-overs
and those boys not yet grown
into their bodies' awkward scaffolding.
From the gas station and the diner, they stared.
The sun shrank them all, washed away
the lines between a Coke can, a pump handle,
and a man's slack hands.

She'd been back a week, stealing up and down
the outside stairs of her apartment at the grocery.
Tired of passing through men who stood like flint,
she longed to wear red, to leave a scarlet smudge
on a glass or napkin, to strike a little fire
from hands as still as fieldstones.

At twilight, she sat on the stairs
and watched the world dissolve.
Wrapped in a nightgown the color of robins' eggs,
she lit a cigarette, imagined herself a starlet
waiting for roomservice and a cold martini.
New York, Paris, New Orleans —
to be anyplace where the day didn't end
in cold cream, a warm bath, television.

White clapboard surrendered the sun,
became skeletal, until she swam among the bones
of a drowned town. She flipped the cigarette into the dark
and thought about the men she'd known,
how an August night can lift a weight of years,
how she could almost imagine innocence again.

Words Like Water

She sent postcards of lacquered fruits,
olives, roses, and views of the Pacific coast
wet with scythes of foam incandescent
against black cliffs. Color substituted
for emotion, she wrote words
inked in reds and greens.

She sent photographs of her trip.
San Francisco, Port of Saint Joe —
sand and water jungled with kelp and flotsam.
In the pictures she smiles, a storm-line
and tide arrested in the background.
He's waited for months for her return.

When she arrives, they smile, say nothing.
Fall leaves scuttle across the porch
and circle their feet like papery crabs
fleeing the sound of surf in the trees.

After the Restraining Order

— *Virgil's Rondelet*

Virgil is still
The frog-boy and skulks near town.
Virgil is still
And watches girls with cherry nails kill
Time in empty lots with green boys. Crowned
With smoldering dusk and thistledown,
Virgil is still.

Brucker at The Kudzu Kitten

In a rusting Quonset hut
that shoulders the Mississippi night,
Brucker watches the girls.
It's their legs that dazzle him.
Delicate as tracing paper,
the pale lines of calf and thigh
sketch a blueprint of appetite
against a faded canvas backdrop.
If he had language for this,
he'd call it hope or loss.

He runs a thumb up the spine
of the travel guide in his pocket
and thinks of the slow coasts
of Malta and Sicily. The bookstore
where he'd bought it comes unmoored
in his mind, and he imagines
a frangible house of words,
a place where every wall
is made of shivering pages,
and the letters on the ceiling
become the stars in negative.

Brucker walks outside
and calls a woman he barely knows.
As the night swallows his voice,
he looks up, searching the sky for words.

Reading Hamlet *in Lit 101*

In fresh-pressed jeans, an Oxford shirt, and tie,
He smiled too quickly at every upward glance
From his professor. Those smiles, she thought, came
Unholstered fast as desperados' guns

And took a bead on her ankles, legs, and eyes.
Behind glasses thin as eggshell, he made
The most unlikely Hamlet who'd ever played
The part — a chipper Dane, all teeth and fresh-

Scrubbed skin. Beguiled by lovely words and lanced
By beauty, he saw her now, she knew, as sad
Ophelia, and he the dashing, lovestruck swain.
Too bad, she thought, he never read the end
And learned that poison leaves the heart undone,
That water drowns the ones in lovers' dress.

Confessions

With all this talk of muses, I confess
I've got a dirty little secret too.
My sexless, broken-winged, unfriendly muse
Is hard to find, hiding, as it does, alone
In alleys filled with garbage spilled from bags
That split like overripe peaches or pears.
It hunches like a vulture over blue
Sterno flames, cooking Spam and playing chess
With no one but itself. Just wearing rags,
It mumbles, curses, rubs its dirty hands,
And waits for me to beg. In glee, it groans
Some lines around a can of beans. With its
Tourette's, there's quite a lot I have to bear.
The trick's to know which fucking words to use.

Diptych

On the Roof of the Peabody, 1942

Her smooth neck
is orbited by moons
of pearls. They sweep
to an apogee of flesh
where her heartbeat
keeps time beneath the skin.

Across the table,
he sits uniformed and starched,
wet hair combed
in precise, oily furrows.
They stare at the table
as she practices her new name.

Their glances intersect
above the glass in hidden lines
of force, love invisible
as gravity. The breeze carries
the scent of coal, honeysuckle,
river mud, and rain.

The Parkview Home, 1996

She and I sit at the window,
ninth floor, looking out at the roiling
treetop ocean of Overton Park. Old glass,
thicker near the bottom from years
of slow flowing, silences the cars
and tree-hiss below. Only the muted growl

of steel carts taking pills and paper cups
from room to room breaks
the quiet. She stares blankly
at the window and the cracked
desert of paint chips on the sill.
My name slips in and out of her mind

like the tide's slow creep and retreat,
and I must remind her
of who she is, who I am,
and what this place is not. I run
my finger along the edge of an old photo
and tell her a story.

Nocturne

Light from the reading lamp tightens its grip,
bleaches the bed and walls,
and picks apart his wife
until all that is left of flesh and color
is a mosaic of hard light.

He closes his book and folds his glasses,
finds his world has come unbound
until he can't make sense
of painted nails, a glass of water,
or the spill of dark hair behind her ear.

In sweatpants and a T-shirt,
he leaves the house, steps into darkness
clear and cold as glacial lakes. Above,
the bare branches of oaks stir starwater,
the creak and groan of heavy limbs
an easy music that hints at oceans
touching the night on every side.

Tucked beneath the eaves of the house
and startled by this breathing shadow,
a robin wakes and sings.
He listens and lets the bird weave song
through bone and muscle,
then turns to enter the house's flaxen light,
trailing clouds of cold air and birdsong,
a coloratura like starlight on water.

Gluggathykkn

"Dense clouds with openings in them,"
        — *Old Icelandic, from* Grettir's Saga

That is no country for cold men, he thinks
And sips his beer beneath the braces, booms,
And sails of a Spanish oak. This Memphis summer,
So far removed from North Atlantic ice,
He pictures Viking longships riding the gloom,
Waiting for a blade of moon to cut the clouds
So that men could clamber up the cold shingle
To tumble sod, thatch, and stone; to drown
The stars and tremble clouds with fires of their own.
To have a word for those gaps — those sudden
Windows of stars and lamping black, of ink
And moon — would be like holding sea-shimmer,
A lens of glass and lightning to make him wise
And let him see the world past sails of shroud.

The Cartographer

A science of inks and rumors,
quill and vellum, Cartesian grids
that net oceans of blank page
in lines as slight as hairs —
these are what he thinks about
over pints of sour beer in Lisbon
while he waits for the steepled ships
to belly through the bay,
each prow folding back the sea
in downy blankets. Sailors, rimed
with salt and starred with scales
from flounder, plaice, and sole,
will stagger to their cups,
and for a dram or a coin
they'll run a callused finger
over the table, tracing their paths
across the sea's broad, scarred back.
Later, slightly drunk and wavering
between candlelight and the moon,
he will imagine those lines
and follow them past sad-eyed mermen,
brine-cloaked dragons, and deserts
of calmed water until, at last,
he finds a jungled island, its sand
the color of his daughter's hair.
He will urge the stylus across the copperplate,
his hand always moving out
to find his own heart, sea-dark and vast.

About the Author

Rob Griffith is the author of the collections *Necessary Alchemy* and *Poisoning Caesar*. His work has appeared in such journals as *Poetry*, *North American Review*, *Prairie Schooner*, *The Oxford American*, *ACM (Another Chicago Magazine)*, and *The Formalist*, among many others. He has received numerous awards, including the *ACM* Literary Award for Poetry, The University of the South's Tennessee Williams Scholarship for Poetry, the Felix Christopher McKean Award for Poetry, and the Lily Peter Fellowship for Poetry. He is the Associate Director of the University of Evansville Press and one of the founding co-editors of *Measure: An Annual Review of Formal Poetry*. He teaches creative writing and American literature at the University of Evansville in Evansville, Indiana.

Water Press and Media — WP&M